YOUR KNOWLEDGE HAS VALUE

Andreas Laux

Systematic non-application fields of the flat rate withholding tax

GRIN Verlag

Bibliografische Information der Deutschen Nationalbibliothek:

Die Deutsche Bibliothek verzeichnet diese Publikation in der Deutschen National-
bibliografie; detaillierte bibliografische Daten sind im Internet über http://dnb.d-
nb.de/ abrufbar.

Imprint:

Copyright © 2011 GRIN Verlag GmbH
Druck und Bindung: Books on Demand GmbH, Norderstedt Germany
ISBN: 978-3-656-10031-7

This book at GRIN:

http://www.grin.com/en/e-book/184878/systematic-non-application-fields-of-the-
flat-rate-withholding-tax

GRIN - Your knowledge has value

Der GRIN Verlag publiziert seit 1998 wissenschaftliche Arbeiten von Studenten, Hochschullehrern und anderen Akademikern als eBook und gedrucktes Buch. Die Verlagswebsite www.grin.com ist die ideale Plattform zur Veröffentlichung von Hausarbeiten, Abschlussarbeiten, wissenschaftlichen Aufsätzen, Dissertationen und Fachbüchern.

Visit us on the internet:

http://www.grin.com/

http://www.facebook.com/grincom

http://www.twitter.com/grin_com

Systematic non-application fields of the flat rate withholding tax

Abstract

Since the assessment period 2009 the treatment of private capital gains with regard to income tax in Germany has been newly regulated by the flat rate withholding tax. However, the regulation in the income tax law envisages numerous exceptions which are to be observed with the taxation. The fields of application of the flat rate withholding tax are systematically delimited. The numerous individual questions relating to the flat rate withholding tax will not be looked into.

Key words: Flat rate withholding tax, § 32d EStG [Income Tax Act], capital gains, income tax assessment

Introduction and methods

The taxation of capital gains is of substantial significance in international capital transactions. Germany decided to apply the 25% flat rate withholding tax since the 1.1.2009. The Federal Ministry of Finance describes the flat rate withholding tax as follows[1]: "With the corporate tax reform law 2008 of 14 August 2007 (Federal Law Gazette I p. 1912) the flat rate withholding tax was introduced as of 1 January 2009 as a new levy technique for taxes on capital income. It replaced the previous method according to which the taxpayer must enter his capital gains in the income tax return. So far the tax on capital gains (withholding tax on interest and capital gains tax) which was in particular retained by banks, Sparkasse banks [local German banks], insurance companies and joint stock companies merely had the character of an advance payment on the income tax which was to be determined by the Inland Revenue Office. With the flat rate withholding tax a so-called deduction at source method was thus applied to capital gains, similar to the method with the income tax. The debtors of the capital gains or the paying agencies (e.g. banks, financial services providers) retain the tax and remit it directly to the Inland Revenue Office." With the letters dated 18 December 2009, 22 December 2009 and 16 November 2010 the Federal Ministry looks into numerous and partly complex individual questions relating to the flat rate withholding tax.[2]

Due to the many individual questions there is the risk of losing track of this issue which is important for international capital transactions. Therefore, the aim in the following analysis is to determine the sub-areas for which the flat rate withholding tax systematically does not apply. The research method is the analysis of law and literature with accordingly references.

Results and discussion

1. Principle of subsidiarity

Capital gains do not fall in the field of application of the flat rate withholding tax, to which income from agriculture and forestry, from trade enterprise, from self-employed work or from rental and leasing are to be attributed (§ 32d Par. 1 S. 1 EStG [Income Tax Act]). In these cases the income from the capital investments also remain capital gains; they are merely attributed to the prior-ranking type of income. According to § 43 Par. 4 EStG the capital gains tax is still to be retained and remitted. However, this tax deduction has no withholding effect according to § 43 Par. 5 S. 2 EStG as the tax

---

[1] www.bundesfinanzministerium.de

[2] Published in the Federal Tax Gazette 2010 I p. 79 and Federal Tax Gazette I 2010 p. 91 or for download www.bundesfinanzministerium.de. With regard to individual questions relating to the flat rate withholding tax cf. Loy, Hartmut, The Taxation of Capital Gains, Seminar of the Beck Academy AWS, Oberursel 2009. critical with regard the BMF letter dated 22 December 2009 cf. Reislhuber, Andre and Friedrich Bacmeister, Further selected aspects of the new BMF application letter concerning the flat rate

deducted at source only has an advance payment function as the income according to § 25 Par. 1 EStG are to be included in the assessment and are to be subjected to the individual income tax rate of the taxpayer.

2.

2.2 Exceptions from the flat rate withholding tax according to § 32d Par. 2 EStG

2.2.1 Exceptions for capital investments within the meaning of § 20 Par. 1 No. 4 and 7 EStG

Possible structural abuses for interest income and for profit shares of the dormant shareholder are to be avoided by § 32d Par. 2 No. 1 EStG.[3] The investor should not be able to specifically use the existing differences in tax rate levels between his individual income tax rate and the withholding tax rate of 25 % to reduce his tax burden.

Income from dormant participations and profit participating loans also fall under § 32d Par. 2 No. 1 EStG as well as the income from other capital claims of all kinds (e.g. interest from loans to spouses, shareholder loans, bank deposits). These also include income from the sale, redemption or assignment of the capital claim or the dormant share.

Such capital gains must be included in the income tax assessment. The withholding effect of the tax deduction is to be refused accordingly, if first of all creditors and debtors are closely associated persons, secondly if the capital provider holds at least 10% of the shares in the paying joint stock company or cooperative; this also applies if the creditor of the capital gains is a person who is closely associated with the

---

withholding tax, German Tax Law 2010, p. 684.

[3] Cf. Behrens/Renner, restrictions to the field of application of the flat rate withholding tax in order to avoid abuse according to § 32 d EStG, The Business Consultant 2008, p.2319

shareholders, who holds at least 10% of the shares, or if thirdly a third party owes the capital gains, who on his part handed over capital to a plant of the investor – so-called Back-to-back financings.

However, it is unclear how the term "closely associated persons" is exactly to be interpreted. To be taken into consideration could be an interpretation according to § 1 Par. 2 Foreign Transaction Tax Act or according to § 15 Fiscal Code; a statutory clarification is desirable.[4]

The legislator excludes the cases of the so-called recourse financing (Back-to-back financings) from the flat rate withholding tax. This way the structural abuse by involving third parties is to be prevented. Back-to-back financings are typically so-called single-bank cases in which the investor maintains a deposit at one bank and the same bank at the same time grants a loan to his business. Covered are however also so-called double bank cases, for example if a financing bank can take recourse to deposits of a shareholder, who holds at least 10 % of the shares, at another credit institution as collateral in order to service a corporate loan. However, a Back-to-back financing only exists if the capital investment is connected with a provision of capital to a business of the investor. When specifying this pre-requisite the legislator intended to comply with the house bank principle: Entrepreneurs should not be forced to process their private capital investments and their company loans at different banks.

A connection between private capital investment and borrowing of capital by a company can be assumed according to § 32d Par. 2 No. 1 lit. c S. 3 EStG if the capital investment and the provision of capital are based on a so-called standard plan. This is in particular to be assumed if there is a close time connection or the respective interest agreements are linked with each other. A connection which is detrimental to tax is on

---

[4] cf. Fischer, Carola, Problem fields with the flat rate withholding tax, German tax law 2007, p.1898.

the other hand not to be assumed according to § 32d Par. 2 No. 1 lit. c S. 5 EStG if the interest agreements which were reached are customary for the market or no benefit results for the taxpayer from the application of the flat rate withholding tax of 25%. In these cases the flat rate withholding tax on the capital gains continues to apply.

If the pre-requisites of § 32d Par. 2 No. 1 EStG exist this will result in the legal consequence that firstly the corresponding capital gains are to be taxed with the individual tax rate of the investor, secondly the income from capital assets are included in the general computation base of the income tax, thirdly in this respect income-related expenses in connection with the capital investment and losses from the capital investments can be asserted according to general principles [5] and fourthly the savers flat rate amount will not be applied on the other hand.

2.2.2 Exceptions for capital investments within the meaning of § 20 Par. 1 No. 6 EStG

Income from life insurances is also principally subject to the flat rate withholding tax from 1.1.2009. One exception exists however especially for the event that the insurance benefit is paid out after attaining the age of 60 and after the expiry of twelve years after conclusion of the contract, § 32d Par. 2 No. 2 EStG. In this case only half of the difference between the insurance benefit and the paid premiums is liable to tax, §20 Par. 1 No. 6 S. 2 EStG.

As a legal consequence the capital gains is subject to the individual income tax tariff

---

[5] An income-related expenses deduction is excluded with the application of the flat rate withholding tax. With regard to misgivings under procedural law cf. Kämmerer, Bodo, flat rate withholding tax and the ban on income-related expenses deduction, German Tax Law 2010, p.27. cf. also proceedings pending at the Finance Court Münster (file no. 6 K 1847/10 E).

and will be included in the general computation base of the income tax. Actual income-related expenses remain out of consideration; they are replaced by the savers flat rate amount.

2.2.3 Exceptions for capital investments within the meaning of § 20 Par. 1 No. 1 and 2 EStG

Dividends and payments due to the liquidation of a joint stock company or due to an effective capital reduction are not subject to the flat rate withholding tax at the application of the taxpayer if he holds at least 25 % of the shares in the distributing joint stock company or holds at least 1 % of the shares of the distributing joint stock company and works professionally for this company, e.g. as managing director, § 32d Par. 2 No. 3 S. 1 EStG.

If the pre-requisites of § 32d Par. 2 No 3 EStG exist this will result in the legal consequence that firstly the capital gains are subject to the individual tax rate, that they secondly are included in the general computation base of the income tax, thirdly the partial income procedure does apply as an exception, because § 32d Par. 2 No. 3 S. 2 EStG deems the restriction to the partial income procedure contained in § 3 No. 40 S. 2 EStG out of force and fourthly actually incurred income-related costs are to be taken into account, the savers flat rate amount on the other hand not, because § 20 Par. 9 EStG is deemed out of force.

2.3 Assessment according to § 32d Par. 3 EStG

Insofar as the capital gains tax is retained and remitted from capital gains in the correct amount the tax claim has been satisfied in full within the framework of the withholding effect of the tax deduction and the capital gains must principally no longer be entered in the income tax return. However, if the taxpayer does not file an application for retention of the church tax which is to be levied in the tax deduction proceedings he is obliged according to § 51a Par. 2d S. 3 EStG to declare his capital income.[6] The church tax is then levied subsequently within the framework of the assessment.[7] § 32d Par. 3 EStG substantiates the assessment obligation insofar as individual capital gain were not subject to the capital gains tax deduction in the domestic country. The capital investor does not have to declare all of his capital gains, but only those which were not yet subjected to the German capital gains tax. These capital gains are also to be taxed separately with the special tax rate of 25 % in the assessment proceedings, are to be taxed separately from the other income and the income-related expenses deduction is excluded.

2.4 Assessment according to § 32d Par. 4 EStG

Owing to the unavoidable weaknesses of the tax deduction procedure § 32d Par. 4 EStG recognises a justified interest of the taxpayer in a corrective assessment. These weaknesses include the limited capacities concerning the clarification of facts. The parties obliged to carry out the tax deduction (primarily credit institutions and joint stock companies) can and should not employ any personnel in order to comprehensively determine the facts. In addition, capital investors can not always effectively distribute their exemption orders for capital gains. The same rules apply as with an assessment according to Par. 3; § 32d Par. 4 in conjunction with Par. 3 S. 2 EStG. The capital investor must not declare all of his capital gains, but only those with which he is endeavouring to achieve a correction to the capital gains tax deduction.

---

[6] cf. Lühn, assessment obligation despite flat rate withholding tax, The Tax Advisor 2008, p. 291

[7] cf. Kussmaul, Meyering, flat rate withholding tax: The handling of the church tax based on the example of interest income and dividends, German Tax Law 2008, p. 2298

The legislator in particular envisages the option according to § 32d Par. 4 EStG (so-called small assessment option) for the following cases:

- The saver flat rate amount was not fully exhausted within the framework of the tax deducted at source. This happens in particular if the investor has to distribute his exemption orders for capital gains over several parties obliged to deduction.

- A loss incurred within the calendar year or carried forward by a credit institution from the previous year was not yet completely offset against positive capital gains within the framework of the capital gains tax deduction. A certificate of the not yet compensated for loss by the credit institution is necessary here in order to prevent that the losses which are now to be taken into consideration in the assessment proceedings are also still taken into consideration with the calculation of the capital gains tax deduction in the following years, §§ 20 Par. 6 S. 6; 43a Par. 3 S. 4 EStG. The certificate presumes an irrevocable application of the capital investor, which has to be filed by the 15 December of the current year. A loss carried forward which remains at the end of an assessment period is to be determined separately, §§ 20 Par. 6 S. 4; § 10d Par. 4 EStG.

- A determined not yet offset loss carried forward exists. This can be offset against positive capital gains of the actual assessment period with an application for assessment.

- Offsettable foreign taxes were not yet taken into consideration within the framework of the capital gains tax deduction. This can be subsequently carried out by a application for assessment of the capital income.

2.5   Assessment according to § 32d Par. 6 EStG

Described as large assessment option is the possibility granted to the capital investor according to § 32d Par. 6 EStG if his individual income tax tariff is less than 25 %. An examination of that which is more favourable will be carried out by the financial authorities so that the assessment with regard to the capital income is really only carried out if this is beneficial for the taxpayer. Notwithstanding the assessments according to § 32d Par. 3 and 4 EStG the individual tax rate is applied here. Accordingly the income from capital assets is included in the total of the income and the income which is to be taxed. However, the deduction of actually incurred income-related expenses and the application of the partial income procedure remain excluded, §20 Par. 9 S. 1 EStG. Notwithstanding the assessments according to § 32d Par. 3 and 4 EStG all capital gains are to be included in the income tax assessment here.

Summary

The analysis of the Income Tax Act and the established literature shows that the systematic non-application fields of the flat rate withholding tax can be derived from the principle of subsidiarity (Point 1.), from associated exceptions such as e.g. owing to potential structural abuse (Point 2.2.1) and exceptions with life insurances (Point 2.2.2) and certain dividends (Point 2.2.3).

Insofar as the capital gains tax is retained and remitted in the correct amount from capital gains the capital gains principally no longer have to be entered in the income tax return within the framework of the withholding effect of the tax deduction. Systematically applicable exceptions in this respect exist in the fields of church tax (Point 2.3), in particular savers allowance, losses carried forward, offsettable foreign taxes (Point 2.4) and the examination of that which is more favourable with an income tax rate which is less than 25 % (Point 2.5).

The partial areas for which the flat rate withholding tax systematically does not apply can therefore be understood to a large extent at first glance. However, there are numerous questions relating to application even in these partial areas. In addition, there are a great deal of individual questions relating to the flat rate withholding tax. Thus, there is still the risk of losing track of this issue which is important for Germany in international capital transactions. Fiscal law which is not transparent does not attract any capital investors to German on an international comparison.

References

Federal Ministry of Finance, homepage of the Federal Ministry of Finance www.bundesfinanzministerium.de.

Behrens, Stefan and Georg Renner, Beschränkung des Anwendungsbereiches der Abgeltungsteuer zur Missbrauchsvermeidung nach § 32 d EStG, Der Betriebsberater 2008, p.2319, ISSN 0340-7918. [Restriction to the field of application of the flat rate withholding tax in order to avoid abuse according to § 32 d EStG, The Business Consultant]

Fischer, Carola, Problemfelder bei der Abgeltungsteuer, Deutsches Steuerrecht 2007, p.1898, ISSN 0949-7676. [Problem fields with the flat rate withholding tax, German Tax Law]

Lühn, Tim, Veranlagungspflicht trotz Abgeltungsteuer, Der Steuerberater 2008, p. 291, ISSN 0049-223x. [Assessment obligation despite flat rate withholding tax, The Tax Adviser]

Kämmerer, Bodo, Abgeltungsteuer und das Verbot des Werbungskostenabzugs, Deutsches Steuerrecht 2010, p.27, ISSN 0949-7676. [Flat rate withholding tax and the ban on income-related expenses deduction]

Kussmaul, Heinz und Stephan Meyering, Abgeltungsteuer: Der Umgang mit der Kirchensteuer am Beispiel von Zinseinnahmen und Dividenden, Deutsches Steuerrecht 2008, p. 2298, ISSN 0949-7676. [Flat rate withholding tax: The handling of the church tax based on the example of interest income and dividends, German Tax Law]

Loy, Hartmut, Die Besteuerung von Kapitalerträgen, Seminar der Beckakademie AWS, Oberursel 2010. [The Taxation of Capital Gains, Seminar of the Beck Academy]

Reislhuber, Andre und Friedrich Bacmeister, Weitere ausgewählte Aspekte des neuen

BMF-Anwendungsschreibens zur Abgeltungsteuer, Deutsches Steuerrecht 2010, p. 684, ISSN 0949-7676. [Further selected aspects of the new BMF application letter concerning the flat rate withholding tax, German Tax Law]